Gift

20 70964

CW00506369

THE BOTTLENECK RULES

HOW TO GET MORE DONE (WHEN WORKING HARDER ISN'T WORKING)

CLARKE CHING

Tony

Enjoy

For Winnie, Aisling and Alice.

CONTENTS

"HE'S DEAD."

It's 1999.

I'm at the movies with my (now) wife and I just heard the ultimate movie spoiler.

It wasn't meant for me, but quiet whispers travel far in a silent cinema.

Oh, yeah, I thought.

Bruce Willis is dead.

What a clever plot twist.

We're watching the *The Sixth Sense*, a movie famous for its clever plot twist. It's about a 9-year-old kid who can see and talk to dead people — that's his sixth sense. He's just told Bruce Willis's character, a child psychiatrist, "I see dead people."

The clever whisperer has just figured out the twist: Bruce Willis's character must be dead.

It's so obvious, I think, *why hasn't everyone figured it out?*

Like all good plot twists, it's obvious in hindsight.

*** Spoiler alert ***

I, too, have a sixth sense.

And I'm about to teach it to you.

I see bottlenecks.

Soon, you will, too.

You'll see them everywhere.

Before you read on, though, I must warn you that being able to see bottlenecks can sometimes be just about as shocking as seeing dead people.

When you see *your* first bottleneck, it will hit you like a good movie plot twist does, and you will wonder, "How on earth did I not see that until now?"

You'll shake your head in disbelief when you realise that something so seemingly harmless has been sitting there, in plain sight, sucking the life out of your workplace *and nobody noticed*.

The good news is that you're not only going to learn to see bottlenecks — you'll also learn how to tame them and manage them. Your workplace will speed up and, at the same time, calm down. Taming bottlenecks is easy when you can see them.

I have worked very hard to keep this book short, so that you don't get bogged down in detail, and you get a huge bang for your buck on the time you invest in reading it.

Coming up, you will...

- Learn the FOCCCUS Formula, which is the surprisingly simple process we use to find and manage bottlenecks.

- Discover the five key types of bottlenecks.
- See loads of bottlenecks in action*. (The best way to learn to see bottlenecks is by seeing other folk's bottlenecks.)

We'll start by looking at some everyday bottlenecks. These bottlenecks aren't exactly hidden, but you might not have noticed them. Let me show you.

[* *I've changed many of the names (partly to protect the innocent, partly because they're my friends and I found it amusing to give them funny names) and a good few of the facts (to make them easier and more interesting to learn from). I had the great movie director Alfred Hitchcock's words in mind as I wrote. He said that drama was like real life but with the boring bits taken out. That said, every story you read here is based on a real event.*]

CHAPTER TWO
EVERYDAY BOTTLENECKS

A FEW MONTHS AGO, I was sitting in the front row of a small 13-seater commuter plane at Nelson airport at the top of New Zealand's South Island. It was Monday morning. I was on my way to work in Wellington, at the bottom of the North Island.

It's normally a 35-minute flight. I'd be in the office by 8:30 a.m.

Or so I thought.

We were all strapped in, the propellers were spinning, and the pilot had just given us the safety speech. I was sitting directly behind him and I could see him chatting away on his headset, requesting permission to take off.

But rather than taxiing to the runway, he switched off the engine, removed his headset, and turned around to face us.

"I'm sorry, folks. I've got bad news."

He grimaced.

"Wellington is experiencing unexpectedly bad weather.

Air Traffic Control has delayed our departure by *at least* 30 minutes. I'm sorry, but I'll need you all to head back into the terminal where it's more comfortable to wait. We'll get underway as soon as we possibly can."

He then turned to the man sitting beside me, another regular flyer he seemed to know well.

He said, "They normally land 12 planes every hour at Wellington but when the weather gets bad, they cut that down to six."

My ears perked up because even though he did not use the word, the pilot had just described the creation of a short-term *bottleneck*.

The runway was now a bottleneck because it couldn't keep up with the demand placed on it. Because it couldn't keep up, that caused delays.

That's what a bottleneck is. It's a resource — a person, a machine, a computer CPU, a traffic intersection, a slow internet connection, and even an airport runway — that can't keep up with the demand placed on it.

Thankfully, this bottleneck was temporary. The weather would return to normal and the airport traffic controllers would revert to their 'fair weather' capacity of 12 flights per hour, or maybe even a little higher than that so that they could play catch-up.

As requested, we deplaned and shuffled back into the terminal, our fingers feverishly texting 'Sorry, I'm going to be late today' messages.

The terminal was busy. It's a small, regional airport and we weren't the only delayed flight. When I went to get a cup of coffee, there was a long queue ahead of me. Thankfully, it moved quickly and within a few minutes, I'd placed my order.

As I paid, though, I noticed a long line of empty cups queued up in front of the barista, waiting for his attention. I knew it made no difference how fast my order was taken if the barista *couldn't keep up*. So, I took a seat, browsed Twitter, and waited patiently until my coffee arrived about 10 minutes later.

As I sipped my coffee, I pulled out my fancy iPad Pro and fired up Scrivener, the software I use for long-form writing (like this book). I figure I might as well get some writing time in. There's no point wasting a delay.

I tapped the sync icon and the app started downloading the latest version of my text from the cloud. While I waited, I started trying to figure out how to speed up the airport cafe's coffee-making process, just for fun.

You guessed it— I started by trying to find the cafe's bottleneck resource.

In a multi-step process like coffee-making, the bottleneck determines the speed (and output) of the entire process. If you speed up the bottleneck, you speed up the entire process.

Hmm... where was the bottleneck in this 2-step coffee-making process? (Step 1 is taking the order; step 2 is making the coffee.)

Clearly, it wasn't the lady who took my order in step 1. Yes, she had a queue of customers in front of her, but she processed us quickly.

If she processed us more quickly, then all that would have happened is she would have added our order to the queue of other orders waiting in front of the barista.

So, it was the barista in step 2, then!

No, not so fast. There were two resources involved in the making of the coffee: the barista and the coffee machine. Don't forget that bottlenecks are resources, not steps.

So, which was it: the barista or the coffee machine? I mulled over this for a moment and then realised it was the machine.

Why? Because I'd noticed while waiting for my coffee, that the barista seemed to spend a lot of his time staring into space as he waited for the coffee machine to do its work.

That made sense. The coffee machine was the bottleneck in that process.

If I worked there and I wanted to speed up the coffee-making process, I'd start by looking for simple ways to speed up the coffee machine without having to rush out and buy a second machine or a new faster one.

A few tweaks in the right place often make a surprisingly big difference. Often, those tweaks are just sitting there waiting to be found.

With that little thought experiment out of the way, I turned my attention back to my iPad and noticed that Dropbox was still downloading my book's files.

Huh?! What's up? Normally, the download is much faster than that.

I poked around and soon realised what was going on:

earlier in the day, while I was waiting to board the aircraft, I decided to save my mobile data allowance and connect to the airport's Wi-Fi instead.

The Wi-Fi is okay for doing emails, but it's painfully slow for anything more demanding than that. It turned out that when we returned to the terminal to wait, my iPad had automatically reconnected to the Wi-Fi.

You see what's happening here, right? It didn't matter how quick Dropbox's (very fast) servers were. It didn't matter how (blindingly) fast my iPad Pro was.

What mattered in this case was the speed of the internet connection between them. It couldn't keep up. That was the bottleneck in this process.

I switched off the Wi-Fi, the iPad flipped to 4G and the download finished within a few seconds.

CHAPTER THREE
IT ISN'T OBVIOUS

NOW, I know what you're thinking: these three bottlenecks — the airport runway, the industrial coffee machine, the slow internet connection — were all blindingly obvious, right?

True, but not all bottlenecks are that obvious. In fact, many businesses, government organisations and hospitals permanently operate at their 'bad weather' speed, hobbled by a bottleneck that they don't even realise they have.

Businesses unwittingly serve fewer customers than they could. Government departments need more staff than necessary to process their work. Hospitals have huge waiting lists.

If they used the approach described in this book to find and manage their bottlenecks, they would run faster — for free.

But they don't.

Why not?

One reason is simple: the people running these teams

and organisations *don't know about bottlenecks*. Another reason is that all the obvious and easy-to-solve bottlenecks have been found — and tackled — and the only bottlenecks that are left are the devious ones.

It's like playing hide-and-seek with kids, in someone else's house. If you don't know the kids are hiding, you're not even going to look for them. But, if you do go seeking, you'll find most of them quickly enough.

However, there's always one or two little smarty-pants who are not only better at hiding than everyone else. They don't stay in one spot — they try to outwit you by moving around from one hiding place to the next as you search.

The good news for us is that even though bottlenecks are devious, there really aren't that many places they can hide. They can still be found.

I wrote this book to help you find any bottleneck hiding in your workplace. If you can see it, you can manage it. If you can't see it, it's managing you.

The first real bottleneck I found in the wild was particularly good at hiding and it had been parasitically sucking the life out of its host organisation for many months. We found it and fixed a messy situation in less time than it takes to hard boil an egg.

Speaking of eggs, can we conduct a quick experiment?

Here's what I want you to do for real or in your imagination: grab an uncooked egg from your fridge or pantry, place it on a flat surface and then stand it up on its **sharp end**. Leave it standing, without holding onto it or supporting it in any way.

You're not allowed to boil it. You're not allowed to cast

an imaginary magical spell or use wishful thinking. And - to be clear - your goal is to balance it on its sharp end, not its fat end.

It should look a bit like this:

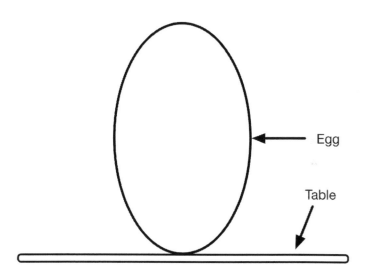

This can be done.

Take your time.

While you are working out the egg puzzle, let me tell you about the first time I tamed a real life bottleneck...

SINEAD AND THE ACCOUNTANTS

IN 1999, I was working in Dublin, helping an Irish telecoms company upgrade their accounting software. First thing one morning, I got a phone call from Sinead, the company's senior accountant. She asked me to run a complicated report for her with the "utmost urgency." She said she'd come to my desk.

When she arrived three minutes later, she wasn't smiling, which was unusual for her. "How much longer is this thing going to take?"

I shrugged. "Ten, maybe fifteen minutes."

"Hrmph. I need the numbers NOW," she replied impatiently.

I looked at her. "The only way I could speed this up is if upgraded to a faster PC."

She scowled.

I said nothing.

She said, "I've been in since 5am. You wouldn't believe the day I'm having."

I smiled, gestured towards a seat. "Try me."

She blinked a couple of times. I guess she was surprised that I was interested. She looked down at her hands and thought for a moment.

Although almost two decades have passed since that day, I can still see her face. She had dark rings under her eyes and looked like she hadn't slept properly for days.

Sitting down, she sighed and said, hesitantly, "You can't tell anyone else this but a couple of days ago, our biggest contractor threatened to walk off the fibre-optic project unless we pay them immediately. We're meeting them in 45 minutes."

"Is that why you need the report?"

She nodded, then leaned in. "Look, there's only so much I can tell you. It's not just this contract. We've not been paying our suppliers on time for months. If this contractor walks, who knows who'll be next."

I frowned. "Why haven't you been paying? Are you short of money?"

She shook her head. "It was okay before we started the fibre-optic project last year. But since then, we've brought on dozens of new contractors all across the country. Every month, they send an invoice and we pay them. The problem is that the number of invoices my team needs to process has shot up so much that, no matter how hard we work, we can't keep up."

"Isn't that why we're upgrading your accounting software?"

"That will help a bit in the long run but right now, the big problem is I don't have enough staff. Unfortunately, it's really hard to recruit people."

"Oh?"

"Yeah. No one wants to work here. It's too stressful."

"How come?"

She grimaced, then explained. Because her team didn't have enough capacity to process all the invoices, the suppliers weren't being paid. The suppliers would then, understandably, phone in to Sinead's team demanding payment. The conversations were unpleasant and were often time-consuming, which exacerbated the situation. Her staff spent a lot of time on the phone having these stressful conversations rather than processing invoices.

To make matters worse, there was a good job market for accountants in Dublin and several of her staff had resigned, which added to the workload of those who stayed.

She let out another heavy sigh. "We've got a bad reputation. No one wants to work here and I can't blame them. I spend a lot of my time on those calls and it's horrible."

I said, "Ah," but I wasn't sure what else to say. "That sucks."

"You wanna know what really sucks, Clarke? No matter how hard we all work, things keep getting worse. It's a vicious circle."

"And it's about to get worse. This fibre-optic project is huge and if contractors walk off, then heads will roll. And not just mine; our CEO's reputation depends on this project."

I glanced at my screen. The report was still chugging

along and there was no sign of it finishing imminently. "Can I just clarify something, Sinead?"

She said, "Sure."

"This is a *capacity* problem, right?"

"What do you mean?"

"Well, you have all the skills and capabilities to do the work, right?"

"Yes."

"But, now that the demand has gone up, you don't have enough capacity to keep up?"

She thought a moment, then nodded emphatically. "Correct."

And that's when my head started spinning. Sinead's real-life *capacity* situation reminded me of the plot in a book I'd read a few years earlier.

It was a business novel written by an Israeli physicist-turned-business-guru Eli Goldratt called *The Goal* and it was set in a factory that was about to be closed because it wasn't making any money, despite having a huge backlog of customer orders.

Although some sections of *The Goal* were too complicated for our purposes here, its plot was straightforward:

- In the first half, the factory's managers believe the main way to manufacture stuff quickly is to keep every person and every machine busy.
- In the middle of the book, the factory manager

and the story's hero, Alex, realises that even though his staff and machines were all busy, the factory's overall output was limited by the two 'slowest' machines — the bottlenecks.

- In the second half, the manager and his staff figure out how to make those two machines run faster and that makes the factory, as a whole, run faster. They ship a lot more customer orders, their revenue shoots up, the factory is saved, and everyone lives happily ever after.

- Right at the end, the main characters get together and come up with a simple process for finding and managing the bottlenecks in factories.

Honestly, I had no idea whether a team like Sinead's could have a bottleneck or not. I figured I would never know if I didn't ask. I also figured we had at least 5 minutes until this report finished, and I didn't want to spend them quietly looking into her big, sad eyes.

So, I skipped past the 50,000+ words that happened in the first half of *The Goal* and went straight for the jugular. "Do you guys have a bottleneck in your team?"

She nodded. "Loads of them. We are all really busy — mad busy — and we're all bottlenecks."

I frowned because the fictional factory in *The Goal* had hundreds of staff and machines in it, but only 2 bottlenecks. I figured that Sinead was using the word "bottleneck" in the broader sense to mean any block or obstacle. I also figured that the only way to see if there was only 1 or 2 bottlenecks within her team of 20 was to dig a little deeper into how they operated.

I asked her to describe their invoice payment process, using simple words that a computer nerd like me would understand.

"It has five steps," she said.

She held up her hand, stretched her fingers out wide, then explained the steps, one by one, tapping each finger as she went.

She said something like this:

1. First, our office junior collects the invoices from the mailroom then we

2. blah blah blah and then we

3. blah de blah blah and then we

4. blah blah and then, finally,

5. We run the computer process that sends out the cheques.

If you're an accounting person, you can probably fill in the details in steps 2, 3, and 4; if you're not, don't worry. Sinead knew all that stuff, so I didn't need to worry about the details. All I needed to know was *how many invoices* could be processed at each of those 5 steps. If I kept an eye open for the lowest number, that was most likely going to be the bottleneck.

As soon as she finished blah-blah-blah-ing, I asked, "Roughly how many invoices can you process at each step?"

"Roughly?" said Sinead, frowning.

"Yeah. It doesn't have to be perfect."

She ran through the five steps, coming up with rough numbers and I wrote them on my whiteboard as she spoke.

Starting with step 1, Sinead estimated the office junior could open as many as 200 envelopes a day (not that they ever had that many).

Step 2 could do roughly 80 a day.

Step 3 could handle roughly 50 a day.

They could process roughly 20 a day at step 4.

And, step 5, she said, was an automated process where cheques got printed and sent out. The computers could easily do 10,000 a day (not that they ever would).

Step 1 – 200

Step 2 – 80

Step 3 – 50

Step 4 – 20

Step 5 – 10,000

As soon as I'd drawn out the little table above, I knew where the bottleneck was.

I bet you do, too.

More importantly, Sinead knew it, too.

I could tell because her eyes widened, and her jaw almost hit the floor.

"OMG!" she said. "Step 4 is a bottleneck."

I nodded, then corrected her, "THE bottleneck."

"Why haven't I ever seen that before? It's so obvious!"

I shrugged. "Dunno."

"So..." she narrowed her eyes, thinking, "what you're saying is that my entire team is limited to 20 invoices a day, all because of step 4?"

I nodded enthusiastically. (Though to be honest, at that moment, she knew just as much about bottlenecks as I did.)

She said, "And, so, that must mean, that no matter how many invoices my team process on the other steps, the only way to fully process more invoices — as a team — is to do more at step 4?"

"Yes."

"That's fantastic news," Sinead said, smiling at last. "I can fix this."

"Huh?"

She blushed a little, then shook her head from side-to-side. "Look, I'm the only person in my entire team who does step 4. It's the approval process and only senior staff can do it. That's me."

That was interesting. Sinead was the bottleneck, not the step. I said, "Oh. Okay. Really?"

"Yep."

"And you think you can find more time to do the step 4 approvals then?"

"You bet. Guess how I spend most of my time these days?"

I thought a moment. "You said you spend a lot of time on the phone consoling angry suppliers who haven't been paid."

"Yes. And, also, trying to recruit people to replace the staff that left."

"And you do those things, instead of step 4?"

She nodded emphatically. "So, if I lock myself in a meeting room for a couple of hours every afternoon and don't leave until I've approved every outstanding invoice, then I can easily double the number of invoices I process each day. Easily."

I said, "Okay."

"And if I double my output, then my entire team's output will also double."

"Great."

"Yes," she said, then frowned as if thinking. "And, if I approve the angriest suppliers' invoices first, the angry phone calls will fade away pretty quickly."

I said, "Yeah."

And that is exactly what Sinead did.

Within 3 days, all outstanding invoices were processed and paid, the angry phone calls stopped, and the contractors kept working on the fibre-optic project. The team had returned to their "fair weather" capacity and, within a week, Sinead decided to stop recruiting more staff because she'd realised she didn't need them after all.

I found out much later that during that time, the company's founder was secretly negotiating a deal to sell the company. They got a good price largely because their fibre-optic project looked healthy.

It's no wonder Sinead felt so stressed when the vendors threatened to walk out.

And me? I was hooked.

During my lunch break, I rushed out and bought a fresh copy of *The Goal* and reread it as quickly as I could.

I then proceeded to spend the next 20 years becoming an expert on Goldratt's work, which is known as the "Theory of Constraints"(TOC), even though I help "knowledge workers" — people who work in offices rather than factories.

About eighteen months ago, while packing my collection of TOC books into a cardboard box, as my family and I prepared to move back to my homeland New Zealand, I realised there was a huge problem with TOC that I felt compelled to try to fix by writing this book.

The problem?

Sinead would never have read *The Goal* and if it wasn't for our chance meeting, her bottleneck problem would have gotten worse and worse.

But before I tell you more about this problem, how'd you get on with that egg?

Is it still standing?

Wait, before we talk about the egg, can we speak plainly?

I ask because I know exactly what you're thinking: Sinead was a bit stupid, right?

That is pretty much the reaction I get from everyone who I tell this story to (though they're not usually so blunt).

Well, she wasn't stupid at all. She was a very intelligent, capable woman. It's just that some bottlenecks are very good at hiding. After they've been found, then they look obvious.

(If you want to know what I mean, watch *The Sixth Sense* again after knowing the twist. You'll notice all of the subtle hints that you missed on the first viewing, such as the fact that Bruce Willis's character never engages in dialogue with anyone *except* the little kid.)

When we know how to do something, it's hard to

remember what it was like *not* knowing how to do it, even if that was just a few minutes ago.

Often, after a few minutes of pointed questioning, the person I'm talking to has their own 'D'oh! Why didn't I see this before?' moment when they discover the bottleneck that's been hiding in front them for so long.

Now, let's get back to that egg.

CHAPTER FIVE
EGG OF COLUMBUS

THERE'S a fictional story about Christopher Columbus going out to a dinner in Spain, long after he'd discovered America. One of the guests said to him that he wasn't so clever because America was just sitting there waiting to be found. If he hadn't stumbled across it, then someone else would have, in time.

Incensed, Columbus went to his fridge, got an egg, then passed it to this fellow. He asked him to balance the egg on top of the table top on its sharpest end without holding on to it.

He tried and failed. "It couldn't be done," he said.

They passed the egg around the entire room to give everyone a (pardon the pun) *crack* at solving Columbus' egg. Everyone failed.

When the egg was finally passed back to Columbus, he leaned forward and then very gently cracked the base of the egg's shell, taking care to not break it so much that something spilled out. Then, he set the egg down on top of the table, cracked side down. It stood.

He then said (smugly, I imagine) something like, "The solution is obvious now, isn't it, my friends?"

This story is referred to as "The egg of Columbus" and the point it makes is "hindsight bias".

I'm guessing you didn't actually go get an egg and try to balance it on its end. I forgive you because, well, neither have I. I did do it as a thought experiment however, and still failed. When I saw the answer, I thought, *Oh yeah, that is kind of obvious in retrospect.*

Sinead's bottleneck was only obvious in hindsight. She wasn't stupid; she just didn't know about bottlenecks yet. After I asked her a few simple questions, she saw the bottleneck and instantly knew what she needed to do to eliminate it.

But there's more to it than that. The bottleneck had created numerous distractions which diverted her and her team's attention away from it. It created angry phone calls that stressed out the staff and kept them very busy. Sinead spent a lot of her time handling the most unpleasant of those phone calls, rather than doing the fundamental part of her job.

The staff hated working there so some resigned, which sent Sinead scurrying off down another rat trail conducting job interviews to replace them. Emboldened by its success, it started messing with the company's strategic project.

The turning point was when I innocently asked, "Do you have a bottleneck?" A few days later the bottleneck, and all the distractions that came with it, were gone. On top of that, though, Sinead — once bitten, twice shy — was very careful to make sure it never came back.

When you find your first (or next) bottleneck, you'll find it was invisible one minute, then obvious the next. You may wonder why you didn't see it before and, yes, you might feel a bit stupid because it seemed so damned obvious. That's just hindsight bias at work.

Before you turn the page, please return your real (or imaginary) egg back to the pantry or fridge. We're gonna need it later.

Now, let's look at another bottleneck. This one is obvious, but only because of the nature of the business in which it existed.

COMPACT DISKS AND PRINTERS

WHEN I TOLD my friend Derek about this book, and about Sinead and her obvious-in-retrospect bottleneck, he told me about the pesky-but-obvious bottleneck that once hobbled his entire company.

It was a printer.

This printer bottleneck wasn't the sneaky, hiding type of bottleneck I've talked about so far. It was a bold and belligerent bottleneck that blatantly thumbed its nose at Derek and his colleagues.

Derek is a musician and back in the late '90s, he created a website to sell his music on CD. His musician friends and other local bands loved the idea behind the website and asked him to sell their music, too. One thing led to another, the orders rolled in and the website grew. Pretty soon, CDBaby was born. Employees were hired, premises were acquired, and Derek found himself running a thriving business. Aside from being a musician, he wrote much of the software that powered the website and his warehouse.

Here's how it worked: customers would go on to the website and order a CD. First thing the next day, one of Derek's computer programs would print a report of all the new orders. Then, the warehouse staff would pick the CDs from the warehouse shelves, pack them and ship them to the customer.

The printer was not a problem in the early days. In those days, when just a few orders were coming in each day, Derek hand-printed each receipt by typing Ctrl-P in the web browser. That sent the receipt to the printer. As soon as it was printed, the picking, packing and posting started.

Manual labour, one at a time.

When Derek started receiving more than 50 orders a day, he hired a programmer to write a script that generated PDF files and then sent them as one big batch to the printer. Here's where the problem started: it took roughly one minute per order, from sending the PDF files to the printer until it eventually spat out the first order.

With 50 orders, that meant the warehouse staff needed to wait 50 minutes before they could start their work; with 100 orders, the warehouse staff had to wait 100 minutes, and so on. And, as the number of sales grew and grew (and grew), the printer took longer and longer (and longer) to print out the first page of the report.

Derek told me, "Once it got to over 200 orders a day, I actually went out and bought a bigger, stronger printer, but that still didn't help! It still took one minute per PDF before it started printing. The guys in the warehouse would be waiting up to 3-4 hours for the printer to print the day's orders. It was holding up everything."

The printer was a bottleneck but, thankfully, it was the stupid kind that makes no effort to hide itself.

So, what did Derek do?

Well, he could have gone out and bought another even bigger printer. He could have kept his current printer and bought an additional printer, but then, he would have had to change his computer program to print out on two printers. He could have come in at 5 a.m. to kick off the program earlier, but...5 a.m.?

Instead, he mulled this over — something we Bottleneckers (and musicians turned computer programmers) prefer way more than early mornings.

He told me he was perplexed. Why on earth did the printer take so long to get started every morning? It's not like it needed coffee. So, he went back to basics and dug inside the printer's technical manual where he discovered that the format of the report his software was sending to the printer, the standard PDF we are all familiar with, wasn't the fast, efficient option that he thought it was. The fast, efficient option is something called PostScript.

Derek said, "I found a programmer friend who knew PostScript, and he wrote a program that converted our orders into PostScript format, and ZIP ZIP ZIP ZIP ZIP! They popped out of the printer in a few seconds each."

That instantly gained his warehouse staff 3-4 extra hours a day.

The bottleneck was gone.

It was obvious, but it's not hard to imagine how, in a

different organisation, it could have remained hidden. Derek told me that, as his business grew, it remained small and tight-knit. Whenever anything like this happened, the warehouse workers let him know asap.

There was no drama, no stress, just a simple "Hey Derek, we've got a problem." In that type of environment, bottlenecks and other blockers were found and fixed before they had a chance to hide.

Can you imagine how, if CDBaby had been larger (and called, I guess, CDDaddy), things would have been different? If their warehouse staff, IT department and CEO had all worked in different buildings, maybe even different states or countries, they wouldn't have known each other, let alone chatted with each other. In a large company like that, the warehouse workers would have likely tolerated hold-ups like the printer because, you know, "What can we do about it?"

I PROMISED to tell you about five types of bottlenecks. Here are the first two:

- **Wild bottlenecks** are often hidden and they're either unmanaged or poorly managed. We find, then tame them using the FOCCCUS formula.
- **Tamed bottlenecks** don't have as much capacity as we'd like, but they are visible and they are managed.

We use the FOCCCUS formula to tame bottlenecks, much like what horse wranglers do with wild horses. Sometimes, as what happened with Sinead and Derek, the bottlenecks disappear. Other times, after we've tamed our *wild* bottleneck, they hang around, and that's okay — provided we are managing them, rather than them (secretly, sneakily) managing us.

Let's get into the problem with Goldratt's work.

AFTER LIVING in Ireland for 3 years, then Scotland for 16 years, I moved back to my homeland, New Zealand, with my Irish wife and two Scottish daughters.

As part of that move, with my wife's encouragement, I culled the hundreds of books I'd collected over the previous two decades, until they fit into one (large) cardboard box. I kept every Theory of Constraints book I owned (of course) and a handful of others. The rest, I gave to charity. It hurt.

An unsettling thought occurred to me. As much as I cherished those TOC books, none would have helped Sinead.

Why not?

To start with, they are all too advanced and aimed at the managers of big businesses (most of them manufacturing-based) who are trying to solve big problems that 99% of the population will never come across.

Take my book, *Rolling Rocks Downhill*, a business novel about using TOC in large-scale software development, as an example. It's a snappy, 320-page read but you don't bump into bottlenecks until page 203, when the wise Yoda-like mentor Craig asks the hero Steve, "Where is your team's bottleneck?" and Steve says, "I don't know."

That's because in large-scale software development initiatives, bottlenecks are a key part of the problem. Still, they are only part of the problem.

It's the same situation in *The Goal*. The first half of the book is largely about accounting and factory measurement systems.

Why? Because when factories find their bottleneck and build their manufacturing schedules around it, they also must change their accounting and measurement systems. If they don't, it doesn't work.

Sinead wouldn't have had time to read either of those books, pluck out the lessons relevant to her, and then figure out how they applied to her situation. The contractors would have downed tools on the fibre-optic project, and she would have been out looking for a new job before she got to the relevant part about bottlenecks.

She just needed someone to ask her a few simple, targeted, questions, starting with, "Do you have a bottleneck?"

I wrote this book to help everyday, ordinary people like Sinead ***find and then manage their bottleneck quickly***, ***no matter what industry they happen to work in***.

To do that, I've plucked the **three most important**

lessons from *The Goal* (and TOC), modernised them and adapted them so they're easier to understand.

- **LESSON ONE - The bottleneck determines a system's output.**

You've seen a few bottlenecks already, you'll see more to come. The runway's self-imposed limit of six flights per hour determined the output of the entire airport. The coffee machine determined how many coffees could be made for the entire terminal. It didn't matter how fast my iPad or Dropbox's servers were because the slow airport WiFi determined how fast data could travel from one to the other.

Since Sinead was the only person who could do step 4 and was too busy with other things, she limited how many invoices her team could process in one day. This book's title — *The Bottleneck Rules* — is a play on words. There is only one bottleneck rule and it's this: The Bottleneck Rules.

It's in charge of your system's output. If you want to improve your system's productivity, you better recognise that the bottleneck determines how much your system produces. You can either manage it, or let it manage you.

- **LESSON TWO - A simple recipe you can follow to find, then manage, your bottleneck.**

It's called the FOCCCUS formula: Find, Optimise,

Coordinate, Collaborate, Curate, Upgrade, and Start again (strategically).

You've just seen the **F** and **O** steps: Sinead **Found** the bottleneck, then she figured out how to **Optimise** the bottleneck's output. Putting aside all uncomplimentary thoughts you had about Sinead's intellect, if you thought the F and O results were impressive, just wait 'til you learn about the other steps.

A bit of advice: don't try to remember these words, just keep reading and I'll show you what they mean. If you're familiar with Goldratt's work you will have heard of his 5-focusing-steps (5FS) and you can check out how the 5FS and FOCCCUS map to each other in the footnote*.

- **LESSON THREE - The 'If Everyone is Busy, we must be Productive' Myth**

There is a common, intuitive belief that the way to maximise productivity is to keep everyone busy. That's wrong. Sinead's team didn't need to work harder to get more work done.

She didn't need to employ more people. All she needed to do was find her team's bottleneck, then think. The truth is that if your team runs faster than your bottleneck, they're just being busy, not productive.

The remainder of the book teaches you how to use the FOCCCUS formula.

[* Don't read this footnote unless you're already familiar with Goldratt's five-focusing-steps.

I prefer the FOCCCUS mnemonic because it's easier to remember and the words are more concrete. And, to me, the words "exploit" and "subordinate" have negative connotations. It wasn't until I read their dictionary definitions that I understood why Doctor Goldrattt chose them, but whenever I hear the word "exploit" I think of bosses exploiting their workers.

Here's a quick translation:

Identify = Find

Exploit = Optimise

Subordinate = Coordinate, Collaborate, and Curate

Elevate = Upgrade

Go back to step 1 = Start again (strategically).

Also, although most people following Goldratt's approach don't spend money until they get to the Elevate step, I'm happy to spend a little bit of money in the earlier steps, if that's pragmatic, but I hold off spending big money until Elevate / Upgrade.]

CHAPTER NINE
FOCCCUS FORMULA

ANDY

ANDY GROVE WAS one of the founders and the CEO of Intel Corporation. *Time Magazine* named him 1997 Man of the Year. When Steve Jobs was considering returning to Apple, he called Grove for advice, saying he was someone he "idolised."

In 1983, Grove wrote a book entitled *High Output Management*. It was aimed at teaching middle managers some of the management principles Grove had learned during his time at Intel. He began his book with a deceptively simple manufacturing example that illustrates the idea and importance of bottlenecks (or limiting-steps*, as he called them).

[* *Grove was a chemical engineer by training, where the concept of the "rate determining step" or "rate-limiting step" is used to understand (and optimise) many chemical processes.*]

Grove was a brilliant teacher and rather than explain bottlenecks using a factory, he based his example on work

43

he did as a young hotel waiter while studying chemistry. He used the example of serving a breakfast made up of coffee, a slice of toast, and a three-minute boiled egg.

He starts by putting a simple schedule together so he can figure out two things: (a) the best sequence to prepare the meal, and (b) how long it will take.

Here are his inputs. See if you can come up with a good schedule:

- It takes 1 minute to make the toast,
- 20 seconds to pour the coffee (from the pre-made pot), and
- 3 minutes (unsurprisingly) to cook each 3-minute egg.
- Once they're all cooked, it takes another minute to serve them.

Most people decide to cook the egg first, then toast the bread and then pour the coffee while the egg is cooking. That's what Grove did. He started his scheduling by looking for what he called the *limiting step*. In this case, it's the longest step: boiling the egg. He places that step at the centre of his schedule, then *staggers* the other tasks around it, doing work in parallel where possible. Total time: 4 minutes.

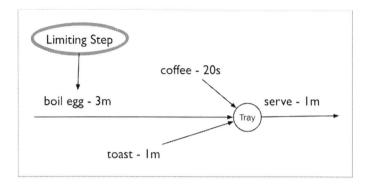

Now, that's great if you're cooking one egg. But you're not. You're in a big hotel and you must feed dozens of guests each morning.

Grove asks a simple question: "What would happen if you had to stand in a line of waiters waiting for your turn to use the toaster?" And then, he answers it: "If you didn't adjust your production flow to account for the queue, your 3-minute egg could easily become a 6-minute egg."

In other words, in this scenario, the egg boiling is not the bottleneck — it's the toaster. When looking for bottlenecks you don't look for the step that takes the most processing time (the egg); you look for the longest queue (the toaster).

Let me make up some numbers here.

Let's say the waiters can easily boil up to 200 eggs an hour and they could easily provide up to 800 cups of coffee, but they only have capacity to toast 90 slices of toast each hour. If the restaurant was only serving 50 breakfasts per hour, then the toaster could keep up. But, let's say there is demand for between 120 and 150 breakfasts every morning, the toaster becomes the bottleneck.

We need a new diagram that shows the flow of Grove's little breakfast factory:

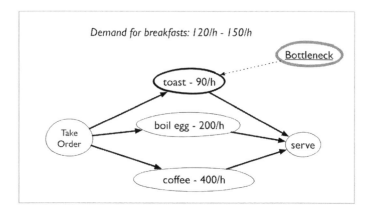

That makes it clearer, doesn't it?

Our conclusion: the toaster can only toast 90 slices per hour. Because the demand is higher than that, the toaster is clearly the *bottleneck*.

*And just like that, we found the bottleneck, and completed step 1 in our FOCCCUS recipe - **Find** the bottleneck.*

Back to Grove's question, "What would happen if you had to stand in a line of waiters waiting for your turn to use the toaster?"

Well, we could buy another toaster.

However, that's easy for me to say since it's not my money I'm spending. (And for all I know, hotel toasters are excruciatingly expensive and that's the reason why hotels charge so much for their Wi-Fi.)

And, besides, when we're looking for bottlenecks, it's

better to think a bit before rushing in and spending big money trying to fix a problem. Over the years, we've discovered that thinking costs nothing, is often quicker and more fun, and is also more powerful than just chucking wodges* of money at the problem.

[* *Okay, I may have just made the word "wodges" up. Let's just say it means "lots."*]

So, let's start thinking by doing step 2 of our FOCCCUS recipe: **Optimise** *the bottleneck.*

This is where we deliberately blinker ourselves and focus intensely on the work the bottleneck does and find ways to "squeeze more work" out of it.

How might we do that?

- Maybe, for instance, the toast would still be considered brown enough with 45 seconds of toasting instead of the full 60 seconds? That would give them a whopping 33% extra capacity *for free*, lifting their 90 slices an hour up to 120.

- Maybe the toaster is like the one in my first student accommodation and has been poorly maintained so only three of the four slots work properly. If that slot could be fixed, they'd get a whopping 33% percent more toast made for very little cost.

- Maybe the toaster is in a corner of the kitchen that's hard to access and an extra 5% more toast could be made by moving it to somewhere more accessible. Who knows? It might not sound like a lot, but don't forget that's 5% increase in productivity for the entire kitchen.

- Maybe we could spend a little money and buy a pair of wooden toaster tongs that the waiters can use to move the hot toast to the plate more quickly than they currently can when they use their bare fingers (which isn't terribly hygienic anyway).

Now, we've found the bottleneck and squeezed as much work out of it as we can (*Optimised*), let's figure out how the non-bottlenecks need to change to improve the output of the entire kitchen. This is where the FOCCCUS recipe's 3 Cs (**Coordinate, Collaborate and Curate**) come in.

People often stop at Optimise and miss out on the magic these 3 steps bring. Don't do that.

*We start by **Coordinating** the non-bottlenecks so they help make the most of our bottleneck.*

As Grove said, "If you didn't adjust your production flow to account for the queue, your 3-minute egg could easily become a 6-minute egg."

We need to adjust our production flow so that the entire kitchen runs at the speed of the toaster. We put the toaster at the centre of the breakfast factory and then *stagger* the other tasks around it. We slow down the egg cooking and the coffee pouring a bit, so they run at the same speed as the toasting, or maybe just a little faster.

Perhaps, they could give one waiter the lofty sounding job of *Chief Toaster and Coordinator* (a title I just made up, to be clear). His job is to keep the toaster busy, to make sure the coffee doesn't run out and to tell the egg cookers when to cook more eggs.

Or, rather than a new role, maybe they just need a couple of new rules? One rule might say that when you take toast from the toaster, you replace it with bread, and set the machine toasting again. Another rule might be to tell the person cooking the eggs to make sure they always have, say, 5 eggs cooked, ready and waiting, but no more.

My friend Leigh, a man who likes his toast extra crispy, suggested they could coordinate their staff's rosters slightly differently and free up more of the toaster's peak-time capacity. He said that if he was in charge he'd get one of the kitchen staff rostered on to come in early, before the breakfast service, when the toaster wasn't being used, and have them partially toast the bread for 25 seconds. Later, during peak time, they'd finish off the toasting but it would be much faster.

I've far exceeded the bounds of my kitchen knowledge here, so let's move on to the next step.

The second C in FOCCCUS stands for **Collaborate**. This step is often the most powerful one in knowledge work environments. It means working together to find out how the non-bottlenecks can help the bottlenecks, without cutting corners.

Often, when they do that, they discover duplicated work that can be cut from the bottleneck, freeing up its time. Sometimes, the non-bottlenecks can do some of the easier parts of the bottleneck's work. Even if they're not as fast as the bottleneck at doing the work, handing that work over frees up bottleneck time. Remember that the non-bottlenecks aren't busy all the time, so they often have wiggle room they can use to pick up other work.

Collaboration (helping) is richest when you are talking about people rather than machines, but can you think of any other resources — people or equipment — that could help the toaster do its job?

I can think of two, although they're probably silly. The first is what I would call a griller (known as a broiler in the US). The other resource that could do some of the toaster's job is a cook's blow torch.

Stupid ideas, I agree. But hey, we're talking about people's breakfasts here.

Moving on, the third C is **Curate**. That's what museum curators do: they have a huge amount of stock they could put on display, but there is only so much display space, so they carefully choose what goes on display. Magazine editors do the same.

When dealing with bottlenecks, we have several different ways we can curate.

Remember that a resource becomes a bottleneck when it can't keep up with demand. When searching for them, we mostly focus on increasing capacity.

However, carefully reducing demand on the bottleneck can also work.

You could, if you were feeling commercially suicidal, leave copies of the Dr. Atkins low-carb diet book on the breakfast tables and instruct the waiting staff to greet the guests with a snarky, "I see that you've put on some weight since your last visit," as they arrive (this might eliminate demand entirely, rather than reduce it).

You could also consider adding an alternative to toast. For example, you could offer freshly baked buns which are cooked, or heated up, in batches using one of the kitchen's idle non-bottleneck resources: the oven.

So, now that we've considered the three Cs, all of which look at the non-bottleneck. Let's go back to the bottleneck and ask if we need to pull out our wallets and buy more bottleneck capacity.

This is the U in FOCCCUS and it stands for **Upgrade**. In our breakfast kitchen, if we still can't keep up despite our improvements, we could **Upgrade** our toaster by replacing it with a bigger, faster model or by buying an extra toaster.

And finally, let's imagine that our toasting capacity has increased so much that that it is no longer the bottleneck. We need to **Start again**, and go back to the first step, **Find.**

We should expect that the bottleneck *will* move and think about where it will move to (and how to react). In our kitchen, as the toasting capacity increases, one of two scenarios is likely to happen: either the kitchen will find it can serve all its guests (so there is no bottleneck in the kitchen) or boiling the egg will become the bottleneck.

In some cases, rather than just follow the bottleneck, we might choose where we want the bottleneck to move to, then make that happen. A full-service hotel won't last long if it can't feed its guests breakfast. If we think more **strategically** about the situation, we'd want the hotel's bedrooms to be its bottleneck, not some silly toaster (or egg cooker, or waiter, or lift, or car parking space, or water boiler ... and so on). That's why our last step is, **Start again (strategically)**.

So, that's how we manage bottlenecks.

I'll expand on the steps as we go, but just keep in mind these two points:

- Find, Optimise and Upgrade — work on the bottleneck directly.
- Coordinate, Collaborate and Curate — ask how the non-bottlenecks can help the bottleneck.

CHAPTER TEN
DELIBERATE BOTTLENECKS

REMEMBER where you put that egg?

Go grab it because we need it to find our next type of bottleneck.

We are going to cook an imaginary breakfast, Andy Grove style. However, we are only preparing this breakfast in our imagination and it's not for a bunch of people, it's just for me. Oh, and we're going to make tea rather than coffee (just because I feel like a nice cup of tea today.)

Without further ado, pop into your imaginary kitchen.

You'll need that egg, plus two slices of bread and a tea bag.

You'll also need a toaster, a kettle, a pot of boiling water, and most importantly, one of those old-fashioned, hourglass-shaped egg timers (the sort with the sand flowing through it.)

Let's get cooking.

Put water in the kettle.

While that's heating up, let's put the bread in the

toaster and boil the water. Also, let's be super organised and put the tea bag into a mug.

While we're waiting, let me share with you a useful bottleneck analogy.

Question: How do you make a chain stronger?

I ask this question when I do training. Some people know the answer straight away; others have to think about it first.

Sometimes, it helps if I prompt with a different question:

What determines the strength of a chain?

And then the answer comes quickly:

The strength of a chain is determined by its weakest link.

We all know that saying. No matter how strong a chain is, if you pull it to its full length then keep applying more and more pressure, eventually one of the links — the weakest — will break.

I ask the original question again:

Question: So, how do you make a chain stronger?

And the answer: Strengthen its weakest link.

Great.

Question: What happens if you strengthen any of the other links?

Hmmm.

The chain gets heavier, but not stronger.

Hmmm.

Do we want a heavier chain?

No.

Hmmm.

I just checked our pot and the water is bubbling away nicely. Can you please gently place the egg into the pot of boiling water (don't crack it, we are boiling it) and immediately flip over the egg timer.

Now, watch as the sand slowly trickle from the top bulb down through the tiny neck into the lower bulb. The egg will be ready in three minutes' time, after all the sand has dripped through from the egg-timer's top bulb into the bottom bulb, via its *narrow neck*.

Yes, the egg timer works because it has a built-in neck — a bottleneck.

Yes, a bottleneck.

The much-maligned bottleneck is oftentimes a good thing.

Let's add another type of bottleneck to our list of bottlenecks:

- **A deliberate bottleneck** is designed to deliberately limit the flow through a system.

So, the toast is on, the water is still boiling, and we have three minutes up our sleeves.

Let's conduct another quick practical exercise while we wait.

Best to do this one in your imagination.

Can you please grab a bottle of wine and a bottle of Tabasco sauce from your imaginary pantry?

Take a corkscrew and carefully uncork the wine bottle.

Now, unscrew the lid from the Tabasco bottle.

Go to the sink and — please only do this in your imagination — upend both bottles and watch them empty their contents into the sink.

The wine glug, glug, glugs.

The Tabasco, on the other hand, drip, drip, drips. It might even need a good shake to keep it going.

(Remember to keep an eye on the egg-timer and stop pouring the Tabasco if time runs out. We don't want to hard-boil the egg.)

Now, let me ask you a question:

Question: Why do bottles have necks?

Answer: To control the speed of their content as it flows out.

If your wine bottle didn't have a neck, it'd be called a jar and the wine would pour out much faster, you'd have much less control and you'd be far more likely to spill it. You do not want that. We all know we shouldn't cry over spilt milk but crying over spilt wine is a completely legitimate exercise.

(Note: One of my reviewers told me that if you ever do find yourself drinking wine from a jar, you can avoid spilling it by making your own 'bottle neck' using a simple kitchen funnel. Another told me you can make your own hourglass or egg timer using two used plastic drinks bottles and two straws. You can Google that.)

Now, let's imagine something horrific: what if wine came in bottles with necks as thin as your Tabasco hot sauce bottle?

The wine would pour out in tiny drips, rather than hearty glugs and you'd run the risk of dying of sobriety.

What if your Tabasco came in bottles with wide necks?

You'd drown every meal in viciously hot chilli sauce and ruin it.

Bottle necks (which literally refer to the neck of a bottle) control the flow of liquid as it leaves the bottle.

Not too little. Not too much. Just right.

Goldilocks would approve.

You might like to think of deliberate bottlenecks as "throttlenecks"*, even if it does sound like you want to strangle someone (and who doesn't, occasionally?). A throttle, according to Wikipedia, is "the mechanism by which fluid flow is managed by the constriction or obstruction". When we press down on our car's accelerator it releases more fuel into the engine. On a jet engine, the throttle is called a thrust lever. On a steam engine, apparently, it is called the regulator. In a bath, it's called a tap.

[* *A suggestion that came from my award-winning musician friend Avina Kelekolio who is particularly good at rhyming.*]

Deliberate bottlenecks are useful:

- If you think back to Wellington airport, the Air Traffic Controllers deliberately created a bottleneck by enforcing the 6 landings per hour limit on the runway. If they didn't do that, it would have been dangerous.
- If you go into a concert or game at a stadium, the organisers carefully control the rate at which people flow in and out.
- The diamond industry deliberately chokes the supply of diamonds in order to create artificial scarcity and keep prices high. Diamonds aren't as rare as we think, but by inserting a deliberate bottleneck between production and retail, the diamond cartel has prevented diamonds from becoming a semi-precious gem. Maybe bottlenecks are a cartel's best friend?

Even more useful is the fact that we can place a deliberate bottleneck at the start of a process, and choke, restrict, or throttle the flow of work into the system so it the entire system runs at the speed of the bottleneck. If we don't do that, our workplace fills up with half-done work that's queuing up waiting for the bottleneck. That's when things get messy. You'll see that in the next chapter where we look at another real-life example.

Great news! All the sand has passed through our egg timer, so can you please take our imaginary egg out of the pot and place it in our imaginary egg cup? And, can you take the tea bag out of the mug? It's time for my imaginary breakfast.

WHITEBOARDS AND TESTERS

SEVERAL YEARS AGO, Alfonzo, who was the Chief Information Officer at a large financial business, asked me to speed up one of his teams of software developers. He said the team was made up of the company's oldest, cleverest, and gnarliest programmers, and their job was to fix the oldest, ugliest and gnarliest bugs in their old, ugly, gnarly code base.

Don't worry, this isn't about programming; it's about our bottlenecking FOCCCUS recipe. If there's anything technical sounding you don't understand, just do what I did with the accounting team and replace their words with blah blah blah.

Alfonzo told me that the team of 16 programmers worked hard, fixing the company's highest-priority live defects. At the time, they were trying to eliminate 112 regulatory defects. He had promised his boss — the CEO — that they would get that number down to single figures by the end of the year.

It was late April, so they had just over 8 months left to meet his promise.

While I was trying to divide 112 by 8, he said, "They have to get through at least 13 a month."

"What's their current burn-rate?"

"10."

In my mind, I drew a chart like this.

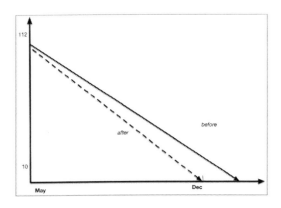

He said, "They need a 30% bump in productivity."

I said, "That's a big ask!"

"Yeah, but look, I'm not expecting miracles," he said. "They're all working hard, and they've already picked all the low-hanging fruit. Can you just poke around and see if there's anything they missed?"

I nodded slowly. "I'm not your last resort then?"

"Second to last," he said. "I've got a big project wrapping up in September so — if I need to — I'll move six of my best programmers from that onto these bug fixes. I really don't want to do that because they're meant to be starting on other projects."

"Okay," I said. "But, tell me, why are these defects so important?"

"They break government regulations. Eve, the team's manager, prepares a report that gets sent to me, the government regulatory body and our executive team every month. Quite frankly, they're an embarrassment."

Later that day I met with Eve, the team's manager. She told me her team was made up of 16 people working in a variety of roles (analysts, designers, programmers and testers) and all of them were good, skilled, conscientious people who worked very hard.

I pointed at her desktop PC. "Would you show me your defect management software's dashboard, so I can get my head around who's doing what?"

She looked at the PC, then back at me, then said, "I can do better than that," and pointed behind me.

I turned and saw three whiteboards. I had walked straight past them on my way to her desk but hadn't seen them.

The boards were covered in little yellow stickies — one for each defect.

We went to the boards and I noticed something was missing.

"You said you have two testers. Where's their board?"

"Oh, they have their own special board, around the corner."

"How come?"

She said, "Once upon a time, the testers' stickies used to fit on the third board, along with the programmers' stickies, but the testers *couldn't keep up with the rest of the team,* so I got them a new board. It would block the walkway if we placed it next to the others. We made room for it around the back, behind the other boards."

Eve popped around the corner and wheeled out the fourth board (the testers' board) and placed it temporarily to the right of the other three boards.

"There you go. That's our entire process."

I stepped back and studied the boards for a moment. It showed a snapshot of the team's entire system and the steps the work passed through. Each defect went through a 4-step process: Analysis, Design, Programming, Testing. (Or, if you prefer, Blah 1, Blah 2, Blah 3 and Blah 4. The details aren't too important.)

What it didn't show was the demand and capacity at each step, but that didn't matter because it did show where almost all the work was stuck.

I smiled to myself because in that moment, I knew what Eve's team's big problem was: she had a bottleneck.

Can you see it, yet? It's okay if you can't; you will, shortly.

I stepped closer to the testers' board, and said, "There really are a LOT of stickies on your testers' board."

Eve nodded. "There are. Our two testers, Lawrence and Anne, are both very good and very busy. The problem is they just *can't keep up*. If we're not careful, I'll need to buy them another board."

I leaned in closer to the board and I noticed the stickies on it were grouped into three distinct clumps: one large clump, one small clump, and one medium-sized one.

I asked Eve about them.

She said, "The defects on the left, in the big clump, have been fixed by the programmers and they're now waiting to be tested. The defects in the smaller clump are currently being tested. The medium clump is full of defects that have been tested and are waiting to be shipped."

I did a quick count. There were about 40 stickies in the big clump on the left, all sitting there waiting to be tested. At 10 defects a month, that was 4 months work.

I drew an imaginary, bright red circle around that huge clump of stickies and labelled it the Waiting Room.

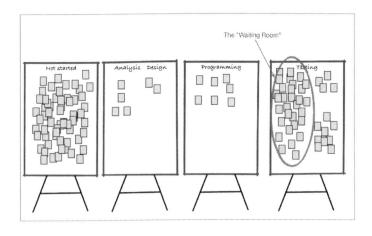

I said, "That big clump reminds me of patients sitting in a hospital waiting room, waiting for the doctor to call them."

"A waiting room?" she said, then snorted. "If it were a waiting room, then they'd all be dead by now. They would have died of boredom!"

She said, "Let me show you," and then plucked one of the stickies from the waiting room. She turned it around, looked at the back, and then blanched. "The programmers started working on this defect 14 months ago."

"Fourteen months?! How is that even possible?"

"It's easy. Let's say it takes the programmer two weeks to fix it. As soon as they're finished, they move the sticky from their board to the testers' board where it sits, in the Waiting Room, for a few months. The problem is, when the testers look at it, they discover it's mostly, but not completely, fixed, so what do they do? They move it back to the programmer's board, where it sits a while. When the programmer becomes free, they fix it again, and plop it back in the testers' board where it waits another few months." She grimaced. "Do you see where this is going?"

I nodded slowly, "If properly fixed, that's good. If not, it loops around again."

"Exactly."

"So, for most of those 14 months, the defect was actually just sitting around waiting to be worked on?"

"Yes."

I mulled that over for a moment. Ideally, the programmers and testers would work closely together and skip all that queuing, but they didn't. Clearly, the testers were the bottleneck. However, because the non-bottlenecks (the developers) were running faster than the bottleneck, they had created a Waiting Room and ridiculous delays.

If we were going to fix this situation, we would want to *optimise* the bottleneck.

However, it would be far more important to coordinate the team better — the first of our 3 Cs — by slowing down the non-bottlenecks. That, I knew, would be unpopular because, no matter how much it makes sense, busy people are so used to being busy that they don't like to slow down.

I said, "Eve, do you know what a bottleneck is?"

She said, "You mean like a blockage?"

"Kinda."

I gestured towards her desk. "Can I tell you a story?"

"Sure," she answered, intrigued.

When we were both seated at her desk, I said, "Years ago, I worked with the IT department of an Irish telecoms company. One morning, I got a phone call from the company's senior accountant, a lovely woman named Sinead. She was normally a really cheerful person but that day, she was unusually grumpy..."

As soon as I had finished telling Eve about Sinead and my first little bottlenecking success story, she frowned. She looked across at the boards and said, "So...you think we have a bottleneck like Sinead's team?"

"I do."

Her eyes narrowed. "It's testing, isn't it?"

"I think so."

She said, "That's why they have that big Waiting Room full of stickies on their whiteboard, isn't it?"

I sat back. She was seeing it. "It is."

"The testers *can't keep up* with the rest of the team."

I nodded again.

"What should I do? Do you want me to estimate numbers, like you did with Sinead?"

She didn't need to for my sake since I could clearly see that her bottleneck was testing. However, since she was learning to see bottlenecks, it would help *her* to get her head around the situation. I said, "Why not?"

Her eyebrows furrowed as, I guess, she thought about how to come up with the numbers. It's not something she would have done before.

A moment later she said, "Well, to start with, given that testing is the last step in our process and the process, as a whole, completes 10 defects each month, the testers must do 10 a month."

She looked up at me, wanting to check that her reasoning made sense.

I nodded.

"Likewise, since there are so many stickies in the Waiting Room, that must mean everyone upstream from the testers gets through considerably more than 10 defects each month."

I smiled encouragingly.

And then she worked her way backwards, through each of the three non-bottleneck roles, estimating roughly how many defects they could work through each month. The numbers don't matter, but what matters is that they were all well above 10.

She nodded as she finished up, saying, "I'm sold, Clarke. Testing is our bottleneck."

"Great!"

"What's next? You can't just shut me in a room and this problem will go away."

I shook my head and said, "Now that you've found your bottleneck, we can focus all of our attention on improving just that one area. If we directly speed up testing, the entire system speeds up. If we speed up any other part of the system, then, unless it indirectly speeds up testing, the system won't go any faster."

She nodded thoughtfully. "It just moves more stickies into the testers' Waiting Room."

"Right."

She said, "Did Alfonzo tell you about the six crack developers he's going to lend us?"

"Uh-huh."

She laughed. "They'd make the situation worse. I can't wait to tell him that!"

I smiled and then nodded, impressed that she'd made that leap ahead.

She sat back in her chair, took in a deep breath, closed her eyes, then went quiet for a good minute. When she opened her eyes again, she leaned forward towards me. "Please don't think I don't appreciate your help Clarke because this does help, a little. At the same time, it doesn't really solve anything."

"Pardon?"

"You've helped clarify where our problem is, although — to be honest — we already knew the testers were our bottleneck, even though we didn't use that word. On top of that, we've already done all we can to speed them up, so it doesn't really help."

"Oh?"

She shrugged. "Look, there are two ways for us to do more testing: one, we can figure out how to squeeze more work out of our existing testers or, two, we add more testers to our team."

She then explained, without using the word *optimise*, that her 2 testers were already working as efficiently as possible.

"Our situation is different to Sinead's," she said. "Our two testers aren't distracted doing other things; they're very focused on testing and they're already working their butts off. Plus, we've spent a lot of time speeding them up and I can honestly say, we've squeezed every drop of work out of those two that we can."

"Okay."

She then told me why she couldn't *upgrade* her bottleneck capacity by recruiting more staff.

She said, "You'd think I could just recruit a new tester. My budget would go up by one-sixteenth, and our whole team's productivity would go up by 50%. Brilliant!" She wrinkled her nose. "Problem is, we've tried that before and it doesn't work."

"Why?"

"Our old, clunky system is staggeringly difficult to pick up. Whenever someone new joins our team, my existing testers slow down, enormously, because they have to teach the new guys how to work with our systems. And we're not talking about a few weeks; it takes months and months to get up to speed. We went through that with our lead tester Lawrence last year, and I don't want to do it again."

I nodded. "Adding someone new would make the bottleneck situation worse."

"Yep," she said. "True, we are a big company, but there are only four testers already working here with the depth of local knowledge needed to work in my team. You can imagine how popular they are! They're working on big projects and there is no way their managers will release them. No way."

She stopped talking then and folded her arms, as if to say *so there, smarty-pants*.

I bit down on my lip. This was a harder nut to crack than I had anticipated.

We'd *found* the bottleneck, but according to Eve, it was already *optimised* and it wasn't possible to chuck money at the problem and *upgrade*. That was the bad news. The good news was that we hadn't yet considered the 3 Cs (coordinate, collaborate, and curate), which are often surprisingly rich.

I looked across the table to Eve.

She still had her arms crossed.

I said, "There are a few other things we could try."

"Such as?" She looked dubious.

I said, "I'm wondering if the analysts and developers could do some of the easier testing work? I've done that in the past and it worked okay."

"It won't work here."

I frowned. Having people in a non-bottleneck role help

the bottleneck by picking up some of their work usually worked very well.

She explained, "We used to do that, but the non-testers hated it, especially the developers. They tend to be so bad at it that they cause more work than they save. Our test manager has banned us from ever doing it again."

"Banned?"

"Banned."

"Oh."

I hadn't expected that. Banned was a strong word. I decided not to go there.

Nonetheless, I looked at Eve.

"In that case," I said, "do you know that old saying about working smarter rather than harder?"

She scowled, because, I imagined, she'd heard that line a few times before and knew it usually came from someone who didn't have a clue what to do next.

She said, "Uh-huh."

"Well, it sounds like you've already been doing that."

"Oh?"

"I'd like to do something slightly different."

"Hmm?" She cocked her head waiting for something useful.

"I want to get your team together and...tell them a joke."

A week later I met with Eve and her entire team in her building's boardroom. Before the meeting, I'd made time to chat with most of team, partly to get my head around how they worked, but mostly so that when we got together in the boardroom, I wasn't a stranger.

I learned that every single person in the team was indeed working very hard, that they all knew there weren't enough testers to go around, and that none of them — not even one of them — enjoyed what they were doing; they were putting in the hours out of loyalty to Eve and the company.

Before that mid-morning meeting, Eve and I carried the team's four whiteboards to the room. It took two lift trips. With her permission, I'd even drawn a big red circle around her team's Waiting Room.

As much as I preach by sneaking up on problems in a subtle and quiet manner, at this meeting, I charged straight in with guns blazing, with a logical explanation of their team's problem.

"The problem," I said, "is that you don't have testing capacity relative to the other roles in your team. Testing is your bottleneck. The only way to improve your teams' work is to figure out, *as a team*, how to do more testing."

By the way, that was when I suspect their eyes started to glaze over, although I didn't notice.

I carried on oblivious. Pointing at the four whiteboards, I listed off the capacity numbers Eve had come up with the previous week one by one, and concluded, "You can clearly see your whole team's output is determined by this one step — testing. Therefore, the only way we can get more output is to increase your testing output."

I looked around the table. A couple of them smiled back politely. All of them looked generally unimpressed.

For some reason I still felt the urge to forge on, explaining how I'd learned this stuff nearly two decades earlier when I read *The Goal*. I told them all how the book was a business novel, where the hero saved the factory he managed from being closed by finding its bottleneck and managing around that bottleneck.

I was on a roll and went on to tell them that I'd written a similar novel that was set in software development. I said that although Goldratt's book had a whole lot of stuff in it about accounting and measurements, sales and marketing, thinking, and scouts, as well as a stirring romantic subplot, most people didn't need to know all that.

All they needed to know, I said, was the core idea in the book: how to manage your bottlenecks. I told them that most people could make enormous improvements by learning just a little bit about bottlenecks. Also, I informed them, we were in an awesome position because we'd already found the team's bottleneck and it was testing. Yay!

I was, at that stage, feeling rather pleased with myself.

But then, when I looked around the table and saw a sea of blank faces staring back at me, I finally realised I'd lost them.

I'd just blah-blah-blah'd a whole lot of management blah blah that they clearly didn't care about.

Hmmm. I changed tack and moved back to my original plan.

I smiled, awkwardly, then said, "Have you guys heard the buffalo joke?"

* * *

I had stumbled across the buffalo joke in the late 1990s. That was back in the days before Facebook, when jokes still travelled by email. The joke is an imagined conversation between Norm and Cliff from the TV sitcom Cheers (which ran between 1982 and 1993). A bit like Columbus's egg story, this joke did not actually happen in Cheers. However, it sounds like something that could have and it's rare you find a joke that's actually funny and also explains a concept so well.

Cliff, the rather odd postal worker, says:

Well, you see, Norm, it's like this. A herd of buffalo can only move as fast as the slowest buffalo. The slowest buffalo stays at the back and the faster buffalo run in front, but at a slower speed.

They must run that way; otherwise, the herd would split apart. And if they split apart, the stronger buffalo would be prone to attack from all angles by wolves.

Naturally, evolution favoured the herds that didn't spread apart. When these tightly packed herds were hunted, the wolves killed the slowest and weakest buffalo. The guys at the

back. That made the remaining herd stronger and faster.

In much the same way, the human brain can only operate as fast as the slowest brain cells.

Hmmm…

As we know, an excessive intake of alcohol kills brain cells.

Naturally, it attacks the slowest and weakest brain cells first.

In this way, regular consumption of beer eliminates the weaker brain cells, making the brain a faster and more efficient machine.

And that, Norm, is why you always feel smarter after a few beers.

* * *

Whenever I tell this story, the same thing happens.

First, there is a burst of laughter. Then, everyone looks around smiling at each other. Then, they turn back to face me with their faces suddenly blank. They are clearly wondering why on earth I just told them this silly little story. That's exactly what happened here.

This is when Eve's team started the first of the FOCCCUS steps: **Find** the bottleneck.

I said, "Do you folks have a slowest buffalo in your team?"

Their eyes, all at once, turned to the two testers — Lawrence and Anne — who sat together at one end of the table, and then back to me. After a moment's silence, Anne, the junior of the two testers said tentatively, "I don't want to point fingers at anyone but, well, obviously it's us, right? You said that already."

I said, "I did," then asked everyone if they agreed.

I looked around the table again and thankfully, everyone was slowly nodding.

A few moments later, one of the senior developers, a skinny fella called Peter, chuckled and made the obvious follow-on joke. "Ha! Does that mean we should feed you two to the wolves?"

Everyone (including the two wolf-bait testers) laughed.

I've told this joke hundreds of times over the years. I don't know exactly why, but there's something about laughing as a group that engages people and gets them into a more creative, collaborative frame of mind. It also helps that the joke gives them an analogy they can compare with their situation. And, usually, that's when I can step back and let them use their collective creativity to tackle their bottleneck.

I was about to ask if they had any thoughts on how to speed up (or **optimise**) the slowest buffalo when Peter, the team's lead developer, turned to the testers. "I know you're both working really hard, but is there *anything* — anything at all — you two can think of that might help you speed up a bit, even if it's just a little bit?"

Lawrence and Anne looked at each other briefly, then shook their heads.

Eve glanced at me and then said, "I know we've been over this a few times and I know you two run a tight ship, but if we could somehow magic up an extra 5 or 10% testing output, then that's an extra 5 or 10% output for the *entire* team — for all of us."

Lawrence, the senior tester, shook his head. "We've been asking that question ourselves for months. But we both work hard and we both work long hours. And, I swear, we've cut back every ounce of fat we can find."

Anne nodded then looked at me. "Neither of us have had any training in the last two years and we never attend our test-team meetings. We cannot do any more."

Peter nodded sympathetically. "I believe you, but do you mind if I ask a few questions?"

They said they didn't mind so Peter spent the next 5 minutes politely pulling on loose threads, asking questions, offering suggestions, until he was happy that the two testers did indeed run a very tight ship.

I glanced at Eve and she smiled back at me with a look that seemed to say *I told you so.*

Thankfully, Anne said, "Actually, there is one little thing the rest of you could do that would make us testers more productive, but I don't think you're going to like it."

Peter said, "What's that?"

"I don't want to sound unhelpful," said Anne, looking around the table, "but you guys do keep interrupting us, asking us a lot of questions about the defects *you're currently fixing* and that distracts us from the *defects we are working on*. That not only takes time away from testing but, after we've helped you, it takes us a good few minutes to get back to where we were and up to speed. We want to be helpful, but, you know, being helpful costs us."

Peter said, "Yeah, I know, Anne, but if we don't ask you for help, we can't finish our work."

She narrowed her eyes as she looked at me for clarification. "I thought we were trying to find ways to make us two testers more productive. If we weren't interrupted so much, I bet we'd gain half an hour back each day, easily."

Peter looked at me, "You don't expect the rest of us to just sit back and do nothing, do you?"

I bit down on my lip. We'd moved away from optimising the bottleneck into figuring out how to **coordinate** the team. I figured it was better if the answer to this question came from Peter's colleagues, not me.

Thankfully the team's designer, Gloria, did just that. "Isn't that the other point of the buffalo joke? Not only does the herd run at the speed of the slowest buffalo, the faster buffalo need to slow down and run at the speed of the slower buffalo. Otherwise, the herd splits apart."

I nodded. I thought of the Waiting Room and that defect that had been cycling around the board for the last 14 months.

I said, "Currently, although you are technically one team, you are running as four separate little herds rather than running as one tightly-packed herd."

Peter said, "But..."

I quickly added, reassuringly, "Don't worry, Pete. I don't know what the solution is. But trust me, we're not going to leave you sitting around with nothing to do. Promise."

He thought a moment, then nodded.

I looked around the table and then asked quietly, "Now, let me ask all of you faster buffalo what might seem like a silly question: do you all think it's a good idea to keep working at your current rate?"

Silence.

They looked down at their hands as they contemplated this awkward question.

Eventually, one of the programmers muttered, "No, it's not a good idea. We'll just keep adding to the pile of fixed, but not yet tested, defects. We won't get any more defects shipped. And, like Anne said, if we keep interrupting her and Lawrence, we will actually accomplish less as a team."

More awkward silence.

Logically, it was clear that the faster buffalo needed to slow down, but for months, they'd been trying to fix their team's problem by having everyone do the exact opposite — work harder. Earlier, I called this the "If everyone is busy, we must be productive" myth.

Eventually, Eve spoke. "I'm going to make this easy for everyone. I have a new rule."

They all looked up from their hands to her.

She said, "Starting now, until we decide otherwise, no one is to work on any stickies unless they are already sitting on the testing board. There is at least three months' work on that testing board. Those defects are, for now, our only priority. Don't start anything new. Don't even, for now, finish what you're working on."

Eve had put a *deliberate bottleneck* in place, right before the actual bottleneck, throttling the release of work onto the testers' board.

There was more awkward silence. After a few minutes, one of the programmers said, "But, we can't just sit there and do nothing!"

I shrugged. Technically, they could just sit around doing nothing. Realistically, they couldn't. There's an old saying about idle hands being the devil's workshop. I wanted the entire team to figure out how to make use of those idle hands (the spare non-bottleneck capacity) in positive, constructive ways. The best way for me to do that was to say nothing.

And then Peter spoke. "You know, we don't just need to sit at our desks twiddling our thumbs 'til the testing whiteboard is empty. There are other things we could do."

"Like?"

"Well, some of the defects will fail testing and we'll need to fix them. That will give us something to do," Pete replied.

Another programmer said, "Yeah, but that's still not going to keep us very busy."

Eve (who'd had a bit more time to think about this than the others) said, "You've all been working so hard, you've not done any training for a long time. You could use some of your down time to catch up."

I looked at the developers' faces, and that suggestion didn't seem to enthral them. They looked glum.

Peter turned to Anne and Lawrence. "I know it's banned nowadays, but surely there must be some manual testing we could do to help you guys out?"

Before they could answer, one of the other developers, who'd remained silent up until that point said, "I'm not doing that. Na-ah. No way."

And another said, "Me, neither."

Anne glared at Peter and said matter-of-factly, "Well, that's good because you're not actually allowed to."

Peter held his hands up as if to surrender. "Okay, okay — it was just a suggestion. Look, Anne, Lawrence, are there any other ways we could help you two out? I mean, we might not be as effective as you guys, but is there anything you could off-load to the rest of us to lighten your load?"

Lawrence looked at Pete then and said, "I don't know, but let me think for a moment."

This is the point at which the conversation started to turn.

We'd *found* our bottleneck, we'd decided it was already *optimised*. We had concluded that (provided we didn't leave the developers sitting doing nothing) they would *coordinate* the team better by slowing the developers down. That would stop the developers from interrupting the testers, which would further *optimise* their time. And now, guess what? We were now considering how the non-bottlenecks could help —or **collaborate** with — the bottleneck.

The goal of the collaboration step is to figure out how the non-bottlenecks can help the bottlenecks without cutting corners. The amazing thing about non-bottlenecks is that they have spare capacity. So, why not use that for good?

Even though the non-bottlenecks may not be as efficient at some tasks, they have the spare time to do more work, which will benefit the system.

Sometimes, doing something *less* efficiently is *more* effective. It seems counterintuitive, until you know about bottlenecks.

That's one way of *collaborating*. There's another: what if the non-bottlenecks are *more* efficient at the work they're taking from the bottlenecks?

Anne, sitting up straighter now, said, "There's another way you could help, but I don't think you'll like it: you could type in some of our test data."

Lawrence also looked more enthusiastic. "Yeah, good idea. Typing in test data takes us ages. It's not the most interesting work, but it'd help us big time if you guys could take some of that work off our hands."

The programmer who'd first objected to helping with the testing, shook his head vigorously. "Na-ah. I'm not doing manual data entry."

I looked at the guy, aghast. Sure, it didn't sound like fun but... I guess some people just aren't team players.

His mouth fell open when he saw the expression on my face. "Oh, that's not what I meant! What I meant is, we don't need to key the data by hand! We're programmers, we automate things like that. I'm sure we've got scripts written that you could use!"

Lawrence, incredulous, said, "You've got scripts that we could use?"

"Of course. Hasn't anyone ever shown you two our scripts?" was the eager reply.

"Uh, no!"

"I guess we've been too busy," said the programmer. (Yes, too busy filling up the testers' Waiting Room.)

Lawrence said, "What do the scripts do?"

They discussed the scripts for a few minutes more and then they decided to take the conversation offline. The programmer offered to show Anne and Lawrence the scripts he and the other developers used later that afternoon.

That part of the conversation ended when the programmer said, "Heck, I can even customise and run them for you, if you like. I bet it'll save you two a load of time."

Lawrence smiled. "Great."

Eve, looking a lot more relaxed, said, "Excellent. Is there anything else like that, which you programmers could pick up?"

Lawrence looked at Peter, "I don't suppose you guys could help us clean up our testing environments?"

Peter said, "What do you mean?"

"Well, you know how we're always asking you guys to fix our technical environments?"

"Yes?"

"Well, obviously, in the past, you've been busy programming, so we'd have to wait for you to finish what you were doing before you'd fix the environments. That's understandable, but that waiting time is dead time for us. It'd be cool if, the next time we need something fixed, you just did it immediately."

Peter mulled over this idea for a moment then said, "Of

course. How about we go one step further? As well as fixing the environments quickly when things go wrong, how about we use some of our newfound time to clean them up so they don't need fixing? And, we could take all the environment management work you two currently do off your hands, so you can concentrate on your testing work."

Smiles all round. "Great."

The developers and testers went back and forth for a few minutes more and came up with a handful more suggestions, but Eve asked them to hold off on those until they'd sorted out the data entry and environment ideas, which were clearly the quick wins. No point flooding themselves with improvements.

She said, "Well, that's superb work, everyone." She turned to me. "I'm convinced that'll be more than enough to meet Alfonzo's challenge. If not, maybe we can get together again in a couple of weeks?"

I said, "Sure, but there's one more thing we can do."

"Oh?"

"There are a huge pile of stickies sitting in your Waiting Room and on the not-started board. Is there anything you can do to clean them up?"

Within a few minutes the team came up with a few simple suggestions of how to **curate** the work (or demand) coming into the team.

The two analysts suggested that they could sort through the Waiting Room defects and group them up so that the testers could work on batches of similar defects. They all thought this would save a lot of time.

The team's designer, a friendly chap who'd remained

quiet until that point, suggested that he and Peter could work through the stickies that hadn't yet been started and identify those that would be the hardest (and most time-consuming) to test.

Since Alfonzo had (rather cleverly) promised to reduce the defect count to single figures, rather than to fix all of them by the end of the year, it made sense to leave the defects that used the most bottleneck time for last.

Lawrence said he would help them and that they should start with the defects in the testing Waiting Room. He didn't care how much time the programmers had already spent working on a defect, he said. Some defects took 10 times the effort to test than others, and he and Anne would be far more productive if they could avoid them. They agreed, and Eve said that once they'd done that, she would talk to the company's auditors about putting manual workarounds in place for those defects.

So far, the team had, with just a little nudging from me, intuitively used all but the last of the FOCCCUS steps of the formula. That step, **Start again (strategically),** wouldn't come until later, if (not necessarily when) their bottleneck moved. It seemed to me that their bottleneck wouldn't move. Nonetheless, I warned Eve and her team that this might happen, and they should keep an eye out for it.

Eve said, "What would we do if that ever happened?"

I said, "You'd have another meeting, just like this, where you'd start by finding your new slowest buffalo. Then, you'd ask what you could do to optimise their work. Then, you'd slow down the faster buffalo so they run at the same speed as the slower buffalo. Then, you'd ask how the faster buffalo could use their spare time — their spare capacity — to help the slowest buffalo run faster."

She said, "So, just repeat the thinking we did here, but with a different bottleneck?"

"Exactly."

The following day, having given the team a little time to get their head around the new situation, I met with Eve, Peter and Lawrence. I told them a story and drew them a simple picture that would help them think about how they managed the flow of work through their team.

I told them about my old pal Gary.

After he left school, Gary went to work for a factory that processed shellfish. His first job was to take the shellfish that had been trucked in and store them in the cold storage area. Then, he would cook them up in a big vat of boiling water. When they were cooked, he'd take them out and pour them into a hopper that fed the rest of the factory.

That hopper full of cooked shellfish was what we call a **buffer**. It protected the rest of the factory from running out of work. Normally, it's placed right in front of the bottleneck, but in this case, it was at the beginning of the process, where it also acted as a deliberate bottleneck.

Gary wasn't busy most of the time, and it didn't take long to cook up more shellfish, but his job was important.

Why? If he didn't keep that hopper full, then the whole factory would be starved for work and find themselves on an unexpected tea break.

On his first day in the job, the factory's manager told Gary that he thought of the business as a big, expensive car that works best when its parts worked in time with each other. The factory was the car's engine, Gary's pile of cooked shellfish was the car's fuel tank, and Gary's job was simple: to make sure the engine never ran out of fuel.

The manager said that was rule number 1.

Rule 1: Don't let the engine run out of fuel.

Gary translated that as: *my job is to keep a constant eye on the fuel tank. If it looks like we might run out of fuel, then I should cook more shellfish.*

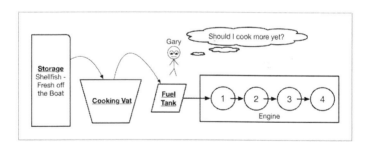

The factory owner's genius was in the fact that he recognized not all of his staff had the broad view of his business that he did. So, he created a few simple rules to help them run their parts of the "car" in a way that kept the entire factory running smoothly. The manager told Gary there were two other rules that backed up the first rule.

He said that Gary should take care to not cook too many shellfish at once because, for safety reasons, the factory had to process the cooked shellfish within very strict timeframes after being cooked. He also said it was important that Gary check the uncooked shellfish before it goes into the cooking vat and remove anything that wasn't meant to be there. You don't want poor quality fuel in your fuel tank.

> Rule 2: *Don't put too much fuel in the tank*
> Rule 3: *Don't put junk fuel in the tank.*

So, in Gary's factory, his version of keeping the buffalo together was to look at the fuel tank and ask, 'Do I need to cook more yet?'

* * *

After I'd finished telling them the story, Eve looked at me and said, "We have a helluva lot of fuel in our fuel tank, don't we?"

I said, "Are you referring to the 40 or so stickies stuck in your Waiting Room?"

"Yes."

I said, "In that case, you do."

We got up and walked over to the whiteboards.

Eve looked at me and said, "Do you recall that the big clump of stickies contains defects that have been fixed by the programmers and are waiting to be tested, the smaller clump are the defects the testers are currently working on, and the medium clump is the defects they've recently finished?"

I nodded.

She went back to her desk and returned a minute later with a large, pink sticky. She picked up a marker pen and wrote 'Fuel Tank' on it, then slapped it up on the testers whiteboard. She moved a few stickies around to make space, then picked up a green whiteboard marker and drew a circle and created the team's very own fuel tank.

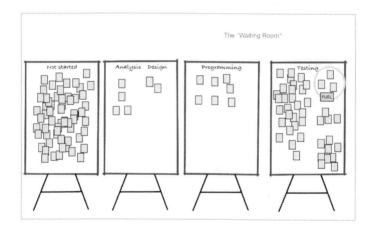

She turned to Peter and Lawrence. "Can you two figure out which 3 or 4 defects we should test next, and put them in the fuel tank? Just make sure they're ready to be worked on; we don't want our testers working on rubbish fuel."

Lawrence said, "Now?"

She nodded, and they started picking up candidate stickies.

Eve turned to me and said, "How will we know if four stickies is too many or not enough?"

I said, "You'll figure it out as you go."

"Right," she said, "I'll keep an eye on that."

We will come back to Eve in a few chapters (her story ends in a way I didn't expect). But, first, let me tell you about our two remaining bottleneck types – they are really important, they weren't covered in *The Goal*, and not many people know about them.

LET'S imagine you've just tamed your first bottleneck. It was wild; now, it's tamed and under control. But, is it delivering the most value? Over time, as I've learned more about bottlenecks, I've discovered that bottleneck management doesn't stop at merely taming the bottleneck.

There are two more questions we need to ask:

Question: Is the bottleneck working on the right stuff?

Question: Is the bottleneck in the right place?

The first question asks if we are being effective: Are you working on the right stuff?

Or, to put that another way, if you worked on different stuff, would you make more money, serve more breakfasts, treat more patients, or otherwise better serve your purpose? There's no point going on a holiday in your super-efficient racy new car if you head off in the wrong direction at 100 miles per hour.

The curation step in the FOCCCUS formula is often the most powerful, but also the most neglected. It helps us make sure we are pushing the right work through the team *given where their bottleneck is.*

- In bad weather, when the runway capacity is cut down at Wellington airport, it makes sense for the Air Traffic Controllers to carefully curate which aircraft use their precious runway now that they've made it into the bottleneck. It's sensible to delay a small aircraft (like mine) that have few passengers and are still on the ground, so they can focus on the larger aircraft that are in the air.

- When you ask your waiter to help you choose between dish A (a fabulous dish which takes the head chef 20 minutes to prepare) and dish B (a very nice dish prepared earlier in the day, that's sitting in the fridge and just needs plating), they will have been trained to favour dish B, especially when the kitchen is busy. At peak times, the head chef's time is very precious.

- Likewise, Eve's team curated their defects according to how difficult they were to test (because testing is their bottleneck) then talked to the audit department to put workarounds in place for the most difficult ones.

I have a name for bottlenecks that are working on the right stuff:

- **Right-stuff bottlenecks** are tamed, and their work has been properly **curated** so they are working on the right stuff.

As for the second question regarding efficiency, it's not always obvious but not all bottlenecks are created equal. A team may go half as fast if their bottleneck is X, compared to Y.

- It simply does not make sense for a hotel's toaster to limit the number of guests the hotel can serve. In most cases, a hotel's bottleneck should be its bedrooms, and all the other hotel resources should be able to cope with the demands placed on them by the guests staying in those rooms.
- Likewise, it makes no sense for one person in an accounting team to be a bottleneck for that team and jeopardise a large company's enormously expensive, strategic project.
- On the other hand, it does make sense that an airport would cut its runway capacity by half and turn it into a deliberate bottleneck if passengers' safety is at risk. It wouldn't make sense if the airport had to limit the number of flights it made each day because there was a shortage of public bathrooms or carparks.

During the last step in our FOCCCUS formula, Start Again (strategically), we think about whether the bottleneck is in the right place.

Let's name our last type of bottleneck.

- **Right-place bottlenecks** are not only tamed, but they are where they're supposed to be.

And now, let's see an example of a right-place bottleneck that saves lives.

THE ENGLISH PATIENTS

I FIRST HEARD of Italian orthopaedic surgeon John Petri back in 2005 when he made a brief appearance in the UK headlines because he had reduced his waiting lists by using an unconventional "dual operating" system.

The dual-operating system works like this: while Petri operates on patient A, his team prepares patient B in the theatre next door. As soon as he's completed his part of patient A's operation, he hands over to a junior doctor to wrap things up, then moves next door to starts operating on patient B, and so on.

The dual-operating system is commonly used in French hospitals (where Petri had previously worked) but it wasn't used in UK hospitals.

That's not the only difference between the two countries' medical systems.

The UK hospitals also had these things called "waiting lists."

Petri said that when he told his wife, who is French, about the waiting lists, she didn't understand.

He said, "She knew you could get stuck on a liste d'attente while desperately trying to reach a representative of the French bureaucracy over the phone, but a surgical liste d'attente? She was horrified."

So was Petri, so he sat down and figured out how to improve things, using lessons he'd learnt in *The Goal*.

He soon realised that he wasn't his team's bottleneck, but he wanted to be. Yes, you read that right: *he* wanted to be the bottleneck because the bottleneck was in the wrong place.

"If you were running a factory, you wouldn't allow your most important and most expensive machine to stand idle. The same is true in a hospital," he told *The Times*.

So, where was the bottleneck? It was the theatre capacity. Petri had one theatre. He needed two.

Since the patients were both prepared and operated on in the same theatre, that meant a lot of down time for him. If he could somehow find more theatre capacity, he could increase the number of patients his team treated.

So, he and his team used their existing theatre capacity better by working in 5-hour sessions, rather than the standard 3.5. The theatre was previously sitting idle during those 1.5 hours, so it cost nothing. In FOCCCUS terms, he **optimised** his use of the bottleneck.

That helped.

But it didn't help enough.

He still had a waiting list.

So, he sat down and wrote a business case asking his

hospital's CEO to have a new operating theatre built, so they could start using the dual operating system. He and his colleagues visited a similar French hospital to learn how they worked. The CEO liked the idea, and they built a second operating theatre.

Let's think about that for a moment. Would an extra theatre, on its own, be enough? If you're going to operate in one theatre and prepare patients in another theatre, don't you need two anaesthesiologists, more nurses and other staff?

Yes, you do, and those staff don't come for free. They staffed up the theatres, so every resource other than Petri had spare capacity. Finally, Petri was the bottleneck.

Sometimes, people think that being a bottleneck is a bad thing, but this was a deliberate, strategic choice to **Upgrade** the capacity of the team around a strategic bottleneck: Dr. Petri.

It required a significant investment (to build and equip the theatre) and it increased costs (to employ more staff), but it also increased the number of patients treated. Petri told me, by email, that he and his team's throughput tripled, and they—in his words—"annihilated the waiting list."

WE ARE ALMOST at the end of this big-bang-for-your-buck bottleneck book, and I have great news for you. You now know more than enough to go find your own bottleneck and start managing it.

I bet there's one burning question on your mind...

Question: How do I find MY bottleneck?

It is easier than you think, now that you know what a bottleneck is. They tend to reveal themselves by the long queues of work that build up in front of them.

The quick answer is: Find the long queue / big build-up of work in your process, team or organisation, and then look for your bottleneck somewhere in the process just after that.

The slightly longer answer:

ONE - List the major steps in your process (there will be between 2 and 8 steps).

You can't manage what you can't see, so make your work flow visible.

- If you like bullet points, use bullet points.
- If you like pictures, draw a picture.
- If you don't have a pen, hold up one hand and count the major steps off on your fingers.
- If you already have a whiteboard like Eve's, make sure it's up-to-date, then move to the next step.
- If you work with physical things like widgets in a factory, or patients in a hospital, wander around your premises and list the steps as you go.

TWO - Look for your bottleneck by doing one or all the following:

- Look for the build-up of work (the queue) in front of it. Your bottleneck step will be nearby.
- Look for the idle resources. Your bottleneck step will happen before that.
- If all the resources are idle (imagine a factory with no work), then the part of your organisation that brings in the work (that's the sales and marketing teams in a business) is your bottleneck.
- Estimate roughly how many things (invoices, defects, etc.) can be done by each step/resource each minute/hour/month. The bottleneck resource should jump out at you. You might be able to run reports.

THREE - If there are multiple resources doing that step — such as a coffee machine and a barista — figure out which one is slowing things down.

FOUR - Once you think you've found your bottleneck, try to prove yourself wrong. If you can't, you've probably found your bottleneck. If you can, keep looking.

Note that I haven't spelt out paint-by-numbers style instructions for you to follow blindly. That's because each bottleneck situation is different. You need to think on your feet, try stuff and see what works and what doesn't. It's easier than you think.

CHAPTER FIFTEEN
BUT WAIT...

WHAT HAPPENED WITH EVE?

ALMOST A YEAR LATER, Eve and I had lunch together in a little French café around the corner from her office.

After we'd ordered, I asked her, "How'd it all go then?"

She said, "We fixed and tested 106 of the 112 defects, so we hit Alfonzo's target. Of the six remaining defects, we sent three to another team to fix, and we put manual work-arounds in place for the other three — they were impossible to fix."

"That's great."

"We bumped our throughput up by a little over 30% without needing to spend a penny."

"Brilliant!"

"I ran some stats this morning and a year ago, it used to take, on average, just over 10 months from the time our analyst first looked at a non-urgent defect to the time we shipped it. Now that we run as a tightly packed herd, with only a few stickies in our testers' Waiting Room, that 10-

month turnaround time is down to 5 weeks. Isn't that incredible?"

"Fantastic!"

Eve said, "And, do you remember how Alfonzo promised to lend us six developers if we need them?"

I nodded. "You didn't need them."

"No!" she chuckled. "In fact, it turns out that we had too many programmers in our team, so I reduced my headcount and gave three to projects that could use them. So, not only did our throughput jump by a third, but my budget has actually dropped by 15%."

"Oh?" I said, momentarily taken aback. I hadn't expected that.

It's not uncommon for teams to find their bottleneck, build their processes up around that bottleneck, and then when they notice their non-bottlenecks aren't busy all the time, get rid of some of them.

However, if they cut too much non-bottleneck capacity, their bottleneck moves and their performance plummets. I wouldn't be surprised, given Eve's bump in productivity, if that had happened. But, I still had to check.

"Is testing still your bottleneck?"

She frowned, confused. "Of course. Where else could it be?"

"Well," I said, as delicately as I could, "there is a difference between when bottlenecks have spare capacity (which they use to help the bottleneck improve and be productive) and excess capacity (which is unneeded). How do you know you've not released too many developers?"

She scrunched up her nose. "We're not silly, Clarke. We

were very careful to make sure that didn't happen. I don't ever want my precious testers to run out of work, so we make sure their Fuel Tank always has a few stickies in it, ready for testing. Not too many, not too few, but enough. We couldn't do that if our programmers were the bottleneck."

I shook my head. "No, you couldn't. That's good."

We changed subject and talked about the sorts of things that normal, everyday people chat about over a nice lunch.

When we finished our meal half an hour later, Eve said, "You know what, Clarke?"

"What?"

"I can't believe a few small changes could make such a big difference."

I nodded. That was the beautiful thing about bottlenecks.

A smile lit up her face.

She said, "**My team is calmer, happier, smaller, and faster than we've ever been.**"

I smiled back.

She said, "Thank you."

Eve's comment was why I wrote this book.

THE END

CHAPTER SIXTEEN
WHAT'S NEXT?

CALMER, HAPPIER, SMALLER, FASTER

WANT TO KNOW MORE?

- Join the Bottleneck Rulers Facebook community: https://www.facebook.com/groups/Bottleneck Rulers/ (There's no selling, only helping.)
- Email me at clarke@rolls.rocks.
- Follow (or contact) me at: **linkedin.com/in/tocclarke** and **https://twitter.com/clarkeching**.

P.S. If you need any whiteboards, give Eve a call. I think she has a couple she is no longer using.

ACKNOWLEDGMENTS

My thanks to Russell Healy, Greg Urquhart, Leigh Mullin, Graeme Thomas, Bruce Scharlau, Greg Brougham, Laz Allen, Mark Woeppell, Ali Law, Rosslyn Clowe, Belinda Harte, Rob Newbold, Jay Bakst, Luke van Erpers Roijaards, Jason Cribb, Avina Kelekolio, Ranjan Sharma, Philip Marris, John Tripp, Jan Williams, Patrick Filoche, Paul Mitchell, David Lowe, Bruce Willis, Andrew Sumner, and Jim Bowles.

In memory of the man who taught me to think: Dr. Eliyahu Goldratt (1947 - 2011).

Printed in Great Britain
by Amazon